My Little Garden

"Coloured Bedtime StoryBook"

By

Bridget Krone

Illustrated by

Megan Lotter

ILLUSTRATED & PUBLISHED
BY
E-KİTAP PROJESİ & CHEAPEST BOOKS

www.cheapestboooks.com

 www.facebook.com/EKitapProjesi

ISBN: 978-625-6308-94-7

Copyright, 2024 by e-Kitap Projesi
Istanbul

Categories: Adventure, Problem Solving & Plants
Country of Origin: United States
Cover: © Cheapest Books
License: CC-BY-4.0

For full terms of use and attribution, http://creativecommons.org/licenses/by/4.0/

Contributing: Megan Lotter

© **All rights reserved**.

Except for the conditions stated in the License, no part of this book shall be reproduced or transmitted in any form or by any means, electronic or mechanical, including photocopy, recording or by any information or retrieval system, without written permission form the publisher.

About the Book

A little boy and his dad find a plot full of litter. Can they turn it into something wonderful?

My Little Garden

Bridget Krone
Megan Lotter

www.ingramcontent.com/pod-product-compliance
Lightning Source LLC
LaVergne TN
LVHW070454080526
838202LV00035B/2830